M000211498

# GARDENER'S LOG BOOK

THE NEW YORK BOTANICAL GARDEN

CLARKSON POTTER/PUBLISHERS
NEW YORK

All rights reserved.
Published in the United States by Clarkson Potter/
Publishers, an imprint of the Crown Publishing Group,
a division of Penguin Random House LLC, New York.
crownpublishing.com
clarksonpotter.com

CLARKSON POTTER is a trademark and POTTER with
colophon is a registered trademark of Penguin Random
House LLC.

ISBN 978-1-524-75907-0

Printed in China

Cover design by Jessie Kaye
Interior design by Danielle Deschenes and Jessie Kaye

10 9 8 7 6 5 4 3 2 1

First Edition

# CONTENTS

his gardener's log is intended to help gardeners from all plant hardiness zones and every level of experience organize their activities and chart their gardens' growth, changes, and development over five years. Following the Plant Hardiness Zone map of North America at the front of the book are ten double-page spreads of grids with spaces for entering bloom and harvest times over a twelve-month period. These grids give you a place to track the growth of your trees, shrubs, flowers, and vegetables over a year. If you have a large garden with numerous species, you may need two spreads per year, if a small plot, perhaps just one will suffice.

The main body of the book offers ruled and gridded pages for note-taking and plotting. There are pages for charting what's happening in your garden over a five-year span if you choose. The book is divided by season, beginning with winter for planning, catalogue consulting, and ordering. At the beginning of each season are suggestions and advice from the New York Botanical Garden's Plant Information Service for an average year in the southeastern New York region: USDA Plant Hardiness Zones 6 and 7, which includes New York City, Northern New Jersey, Rockland County, Westchester County, Southern Connecticut, and parts of Long Island. You can determine your plant hardiness zone by referring to the map and list of plant hardiness zones on pages 6 and 7. These will show you your geographic area and your zone and the average annual minimum temperature in that zone. Be aware, however, that even within zones, climatic factors such as altitude, proximity to water, wind exposure, winter sun exposure, and snow cover contribute to the existence of different "microclimates" and can influence plant adaptability. If you garden in an area outside of zones 6 and 7, you will need to adjust your tasks to reflect your climate, and some tasks may not apply to your area. Gardeners in Phoenix, Arizona, probably won't need to check for frost heaving around plants in January, and most city dwellers won't need to apply deer repellents. If you have specific questions about your area, refer to local horticulture experts, such as your state's Cooperative Extension Service, for timing refinements or contact us at NYBG Plant Information Service: plantinfo@NYBG.org.

At the back of the book are short sections on composting, container gardening, pruning, and dealing with pests and diseases.

This log book should become as indispensable as a good pair of clippers. It will enable you to keep track of what you do and when, and, over time, it will give you a deeper knowledge of the planting, nourishing, blooming, and harvesting cycles in your garden.

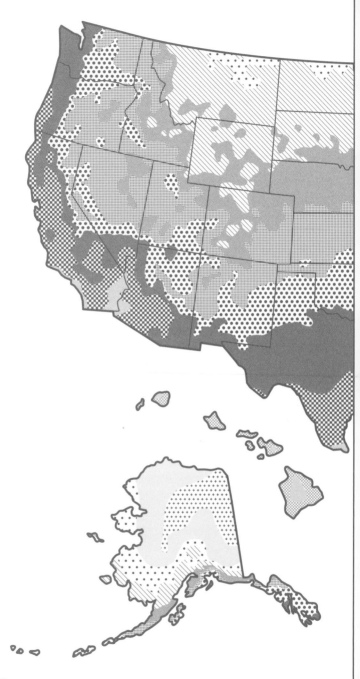

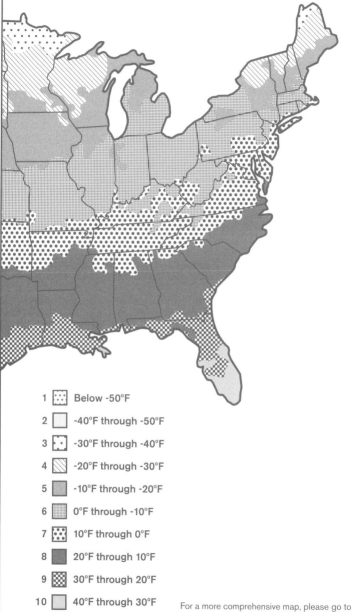

# PLANT HARDINESS ZONE MAP

1 Below -50°F
2 -40°F through -50°F
3 -30°F through -40°F
4 -20°F through -30°F
5 -10°F through -20°F
6 0°F through -10°F
7 10°F through 0°F
8 20°F through 10°F
9 30°F through 20°F
10 40°F through 30°F
11 Above 40°F

For a more comprehensive map, please go to
planthardiness.ars.usda.gov/PHZMWeb/.

# BLOOM & HARVEST TIMES

| Plant Names | | JAN | FEB | MAR | APR | MAY |
|---|---|---|---|---|---|---|
| | B | | | | | |
| | H | | | | | |
| | B | | | | | |
| | H | | | | | |
| | B | | | | | |
| | H | | | | | |
| | B | | | | | |
| | H | | | | | |
| | B | | | | | |
| | H | | | | | |
| | B | | | | | |
| | H | | | | | |
| | B | | | | | |
| | H | | | | | |
| | B | | | | | |
| | H | | | | | |
| | B | | | | | |
| | H | | | | | |
| | B | | | | | |
| | H | | | | | |
| | B | | | | | |
| | H | | | | | |
| | B | | | | | |
| | H | | | | | |
| | B | | | | | |
| | H | | | | | |
| | B | | | | | |
| | H | | | | | |
| | B | | | | | |
| | H | | | | | |
| | B | | | | | |
| | H | | | | | |
| | B | | | | | |
| | H | | | | | |
| | B | | | | | |
| | H | | | | | |
| | B | | | | | |
| | H | | | | | |
| | B | | | | | |
| | H | | | | | |
| | B | | | | | |
| | H | | | | | |
| | B | | | | | |
| | H | | | | | |
| | B | | | | | |
| | H | | | | | |
| | B | | | | | |
| | H | | | | | |

| JUN | JUL | AUG | SEP | OCT | NOV | DEC |
|-----|-----|-----|-----|-----|-----|-----|
|     |     |     |     |     |     |     |

# BLOOM & HARVEST TIMES

| Plant Names | | JAN | FEB | MAR | APR | MAY |
|---|---|---|---|---|---|---|
| | B | | | | | |
| | H | | | | | |
| | B | | | | | |
| | H | | | | | |
| | B | | | | | |
| | H | | | | | |
| | B | | | | | |
| | H | | | | | |
| | B | | | | | |
| | H | | | | | |
| | B | | | | | |
| | H | | | | | |
| | B | | | | | |
| | H | | | | | |
| | B | | | | | |
| | H | | | | | |
| | B | | | | | |
| | H | | | | | |
| | B | | | | | |
| | H | | | | | |
| | B | | | | | |
| | H | | | | | |
| | B | | | | | |
| | H | | | | | |
| | B | | | | | |
| | H | | | | | |
| | B | | | | | |
| | H | | | | | |
| | B | | | | | |
| | H | | | | | |
| | B | | | | | |
| | H | | | | | |
| | B | | | | | |
| | H | | | | | |
| | B | | | | | |
| | H | | | | | |
| | B | | | | | |
| | H | | | | | |
| | B | | | | | |
| | H | | | | | |

| JUN | JUL | AUG | SEP | OCT | NOV | DEC |
|-----|-----|-----|-----|-----|-----|-----|
|     |     |     |     |     |     |     |

# BLOOM & HARVEST TIMES

| Plant Names | | JAN | FEB | MAR | APR | MAY |
|---|---|---|---|---|---|---|
| | B | | | | | |
| | H | | | | | |
| | B | | | | | |
| | H | | | | | |
| | B | | | | | |
| | H | | | | | |
| | B | | | | | |
| | H | | | | | |
| | B | | | | | |
| | H | | | | | |
| | B | | | | | |
| | H | | | | | |
| | B | | | | | |
| | H | | | | | |
| | B | | | | | |
| | H | | | | | |
| | B | | | | | |
| | H | | | | | |
| | B | | | | | |
| | H | | | | | |
| | B | | | | | |
| | H | | | | | |
| | B | | | | | |
| | H | | | | | |
| | B | | | | | |
| | H | | | | | |
| | B | | | | | |
| | H | | | | | |
| | B | | | | | |
| | H | | | | | |
| | B | | | | | |
| | H | | | | | |
| | B | | | | | |
| | H | | | | | |
| | B | | | | | |
| | H | | | | | |
| | B | | | | | |
| | H | | | | | |
| | B | | | | | |
| | H | | | | | |
| | B | | | | | |
| | H | | | | | |
| | B | | | | | |
| | H | | | | | |

20___

| JUN | JUL | AUG | SEP | OCT | NOV | DEC |
|-----|-----|-----|-----|-----|-----|-----|
|     |     |     |     |     |     |     |

# BLOOM & HARVEST TIMES

| Plant Names | | JAN | FEB | MAR | APR | MAY |
|---|---|---|---|---|---|---|
| | B | | | | | |
| | H | | | | | |
| | B | | | | | |
| | H | | | | | |
| | B | | | | | |
| | H | | | | | |
| | B | | | | | |
| | H | | | | | |
| | B | | | | | |
| | H | | | | | |
| | B | | | | | |
| | H | | | | | |
| | B | | | | | |
| | H | | | | | |
| | B | | | | | |
| | H | | | | | |
| | B | | | | | |
| | H | | | | | |
| | B | | | | | |
| | H | | | | | |
| | B | | | | | |
| | H | | | | | |
| | B | | | | | |
| | H | | | | | |
| | B | | | | | |
| | H | | | | | |
| | B | | | | | |
| | H | | | | | |
| | B | | | | | |
| | H | | | | | |
| | B | | | | | |
| | H | | | | | |
| | B | | | | | |
| | H | | | | | |
| | B | | | | | |
| | H | | | | | |
| | B | | | | | |
| | H | | | | | |

| JUN | JUL | AUG | SEP | OCT | NOV | DEC |
|---|---|---|---|---|---|---|
| | | | | | | |

# BLOOM & HARVEST TIMES

| Plant Names | | JAN | FEB | MAR | APR | MAY |
|---|---|---|---|---|---|---|
| | B | | | | | |
| | H | | | | | |
| | B | | | | | |
| | H | | | | | |
| | B | | | | | |
| | H | | | | | |
| | B | | | | | |
| | H | | | | | |
| | B | | | | | |
| | H | | | | | |
| | B | | | | | |
| | H | | | | | |
| | B | | | | | |
| | H | | | | | |
| | B | | | | | |
| | H | | | | | |
| | B | | | | | |
| | H | | | | | |
| | B | | | | | |
| | H | | | | | |
| | B | | | | | |
| | H | | | | | |
| | B | | | | | |
| | H | | | | | |
| | B | | | | | |
| | H | | | | | |
| | B | | | | | |
| | H | | | | | |
| | B | | | | | |
| | H | | | | | |
| | B | | | | | |
| | H | | | | | |
| | B | | | | | |
| | H | | | | | |
| | B | | | | | |
| | H | | | | | |
| | B | | | | | |
| | H | | | | | |
| | B | | | | | |
| | H | | | | | |
| | B | | | | | |
| | H | | | | | |

20___

| JUN | JUL | AUG | SEP | OCT | NOV | DEC |
|-----|-----|-----|-----|-----|-----|-----|
|     |     |     |     |     |     |     |

# BLOOM & HARVEST TIMES

| Plant Names | | JAN | FEB | MAR | APR | MAY |
|---|---|---|---|---|---|---|
| | B | | | | | |
| | H | | | | | |
| | B | | | | | |
| | H | | | | | |
| | B | | | | | |
| | H | | | | | |
| | B | | | | | |
| | H | | | | | |
| | B | | | | | |
| | H | | | | | |
| | B | | | | | |
| | H | | | | | |
| | B | | | | | |
| | H | | | | | |
| | B | | | | | |
| | H | | | | | |
| | B | | | | | |
| | H | | | | | |
| | B | | | | | |
| | H | | | | | |
| | B | | | | | |
| | H | | | | | |
| | B | | | | | |
| | H | | | | | |
| | B | | | | | |
| | H | | | | | |
| | B | | | | | |
| | H | | | | | |
| | B | | | | | |
| | H | | | | | |
| | B | | | | | |
| | H | | | | | |
| | B | | | | | |
| | H | | | | | |
| | B | | | | | |
| | H | | | | | |
| | B | | | | | |
| | H | | | | | |
| | B | | | | | |
| | H | | | | | |
| | B | | | | | |
| | H | | | | | |
| | B | | | | | |
| | H | | | | | |

| JUN | JUL | AUG | SEP | OCT | NOV | DEC |
|-----|-----|-----|-----|-----|-----|-----|
|     |     |     |     |     |     |     |

# BLOOM & HARVEST TIMES

| Plant Names | | JAN | FEB | MAR | APR | MAY |
|---|---|---|---|---|---|---|
| | B | | | | | |
| | H | | | | | |
| | B | | | | | |
| | H | | | | | |
| | B | | | | | |
| | H | | | | | |
| | B | | | | | |
| | H | | | | | |
| | B | | | | | |
| | H | | | | | |
| | B | | | | | |
| | H | | | | | |
| | B | | | | | |
| | H | | | | | |
| | B | | | | | |
| | H | | | | | |
| | B | | | | | |
| | H | | | | | |
| | B | | | | | |
| | H | | | | | |
| | B | | | | | |
| | H | | | | | |
| | B | | | | | |
| | H | | | | | |
| | B | | | | | |
| | H | | | | | |
| | B | | | | | |
| | H | | | | | |
| | B | | | | | |
| | H | | | | | |
| | B | | | | | |
| | H | | | | | |
| | B | | | | | |
| | H | | | | | |
| | B | | | | | |
| | H | | | | | |
| | B | | | | | |
| | H | | | | | |
| | B | | | | | |
| | H | | | | | |
| | B | | | | | |
| | H | | | | | |
| | B | | | | | |
| | H | | | | | |

| JUN | JUL | AUG | SEP | OCT | NOV | DEC |
|-----|-----|-----|-----|-----|-----|-----|
|     |     |     |     |     |     |     |

# BLOOM & HARVEST TIMES

| Plant Names | | JAN | FEB | MAR | APR | MAY |
|---|---|---|---|---|---|---|
| | B | | | | | |
| | H | | | | | |
| | B | | | | | |
| | H | | | | | |
| | B | | | | | |
| | H | | | | | |
| | B | | | | | |
| | H | | | | | |
| | B | | | | | |
| | H | | | | | |
| | B | | | | | |
| | H | | | | | |
| | B | | | | | |
| | H | | | | | |
| | B | | | | | |
| | H | | | | | |
| | B | | | | | |
| | H | | | | | |
| | B | | | | | |
| | H | | | | | |
| | B | | | | | |
| | H | | | | | |
| | B | | | | | |
| | H | | | | | |
| | B | | | | | |
| | H | | | | | |
| | B | | | | | |
| | H | | | | | |
| | B | | | | | |
| | H | | | | | |
| | B | | | | | |
| | H | | | | | |
| | B | | | | | |
| | H | | | | | |
| | B | | | | | |
| | H | | | | | |
| | B | | | | | |
| | H | | | | | |
| | B | | | | | |
| | H | | | | | |
| | B | | | | | |
| | H | | | | | |
| | B | | | | | |
| | H | | | | | |

20___

| JUN | JUL | AUG | SEP | OCT | NOV | DEC |
|-----|-----|-----|-----|-----|-----|-----|
|     |     |     |     |     |     |     |

# BLOOM & HARVEST TIMES

| Plant Names | | JAN | FEB | MAR | APR | MAY |
|---|---|---|---|---|---|---|
| | B | | | | | |
| | H | | | | | |
| | B | | | | | |
| | H | | | | | |
| | B | | | | | |
| | H | | | | | |
| | B | | | | | |
| | H | | | | | |
| | B | | | | | |
| | H | | | | | |
| | B | | | | | |
| | H | | | | | |
| | B | | | | | |
| | H | | | | | |
| | B | | | | | |
| | H | | | | | |
| | B | | | | | |
| | H | | | | | |
| | B | | | | | |
| | H | | | | | |
| | B | | | | | |
| | H | | | | | |
| | B | | | | | |
| | H | | | | | |
| | B | | | | | |
| | H | | | | | |
| | B | | | | | |
| | H | | | | | |
| | B | | | | | |
| | H | | | | | |
| | B | | | | | |
| | H | | | | | |
| | B | | | | | |
| | H | | | | | |
| | B | | | | | |
| | H | | | | | |
| | B | | | | | |
| | H | | | | | |

| JUN | JUL | AUG | SEP | OCT | NOV | DEC |
|-----|-----|-----|-----|-----|-----|-----|
|     |     |     |     |     |     |     |

# BLOOM & HARVEST TIMES

| Plant Names | | JAN | FEB | MAR | APR | MAY |
|---|---|---|---|---|---|---|
| | B | | | | | |
| | H | | | | | |
| | B | | | | | |
| | H | | | | | |
| | B | | | | | |
| | H | | | | | |
| | B | | | | | |
| | H | | | | | |
| | B | | | | | |
| | H | | | | | |
| | B | | | | | |
| | H | | | | | |
| | B | | | | | |
| | H | | | | | |
| | B | | | | | |
| | H | | | | | |
| | B | | | | | |
| | H | | | | | |
| | B | | | | | |
| | H | | | | | |
| | B | | | | | |
| | H | | | | | |
| | B | | | | | |
| | H | | | | | |
| | B | | | | | |
| | H | | | | | |
| | B | | | | | |
| | H | | | | | |
| | B | | | | | |
| | H | | | | | |
| | B | | | | | |
| | H | | | | | |
| | B | | | | | |
| | H | | | | | |
| | B | | | | | |
| | H | | | | | |
| | B | | | | | |
| | H | | | | | |
| | B | | | | | |
| | H | | | | | |

| JUN | JUL | AUG | SEP | OCT | NOV | DEC |
|-----|-----|-----|-----|-----|-----|-----|
|     |     |     |     |     |     |     |

WINTER

## WINTER

**YEAR**

| 1 | 2 | 3 | 4 | 5 | |
|---|---|---|---|---|---|
| | | | | | *Planning* |
| ○ | ○ | ○ | ○ | ○ | Use garden notes, photos, and sketches to assess areas that need plants |
| ○ | ○ | ○ | ○ | ○ | Determine types and quantities of plants to order |
| ○ | ○ | ○ | ○ | ○ | Begin to order plants from seed and nursery catalogues |
| | | | | | *Chores and Maintenance* |
| ○ | ○ | ○ | ○ | ○ | After ground freezes, mulch perennials and bulb planting beds. The mulch will prevent heaving during the alternating freeze-thaw cycle |
| ○ | ○ | ○ | ○ | ○ | Tie and support evergreen shrubs early to avoid breakage from snow |
| ○ | ○ | ○ | ○ | ○ | Provide burlap windbreaks for boxwood and broad-leaved evergreens |
| ○ | ○ | ○ | ○ | ○ | Protect trees from mouse damage with wire-mesh trunk guards |
| ○ | ○ | ○ | ○ | ○ | Protect shrubs from deer with burlap or netting |
| ○ | ○ | ○ | ○ | ○ | Inspect ornamental trees and shrubs for scale insects |
| ○ | ○ | ○ | ○ | ○ | If a thaw occurs, apply an antidesiccant to newly planted needle-leaved or broad-leaved evergreens |
| ○ | ○ | ○ | ○ | ○ | Use wood ashes from the fireplace as a source of potash |
| ○ | ○ | ○ | ○ | ○ | Check on dahlia, canna, and gladiolus bulbs for rotting and/or drying |
| ○ | ○ | ○ | ○ | ○ | Avoid the use of salt to melt snow as it is toxic to most plants; use sawdust, sand, or cat litter for traction |
| | | | | | *Planting (late winter)* |
| ○ | ○ | ○ | ○ | ○ | Take cuttings of indoor plants, such as lantana, geranium, coleus, heliotrope, fuchsia, and begonia, to use as bedding plants in late spring |

**YEAR**

1 2 3 4 5

| | | | | | |
|---|---|---|---|---|---|
| ○ | ○ | ○ | ○ | ○ | Sow seeds of annuals that require a long growing season, for instance, lobelia, petunia, vinca, browallia, snapdragon, and verbena |

### Pruning and Fertilizing

| | | | | | |
|---|---|---|---|---|---|
| ○ | ○ | ○ | ○ | ○ | Prune evergreen branches to use in holiday decorating |
| ○ | ○ | ○ | ○ | ○ | Rejuvenate overgrown shrubs as weather permits, until new growth begins in spring |
| ○ | ○ | ○ | ○ | ○ | Prune storm-damaged branches promptly; this prevents tearing of the bark |
| ○ | ○ | ○ | ○ | ○ | Prune early-flowering shrubs and trees, like forsythia, pussy willow, and quince, for forcing indoors |

### Indoors

| | | | | | |
|---|---|---|---|---|---|
| ○ | ○ | ○ | ○ | ○ | If you purchase a Christmas tree, keep it in a bucket of water in a cool place until ready for display. Set the tree up in a reservoir stand. Cut on a slant about 1 inch above existing cut for optimum water absorption. Keep reservoir filled and place tree in the coolest part of the room. Sterilize tree stand with a solution of boiling water and vinegar after use. |
| ○ | ○ | ○ | ○ | ○ | When buying houseplants in winter, be sure to wrap them up well for the trip home; this prevents the foliage from freezing and protects tropical plants from drafts |
| ○ | ○ | ○ | ○ | ○ | Give houseplants as much light as possible as days grow shorter |
| ○ | ○ | ○ | ○ | ○ | Provide houseplants with increased humidity; mist often or place over a tray of moist pebbles |
| ○ | ○ | ○ | ○ | ○ | Because houseplants grow more slowly in winter, increase the time between waterings, but water thoroughly each time |

**YEAR**

1  2  3  4  5

| | | | | | |
|---|---|---|---|---|---|
| ○ | ○ | ○ | ○ | ○ | On frigid nights, move houseplants away from windows or cover glass with thick newspaper or cardboard |
| ○ | ○ | ○ | ○ | ○ | Clean leaves of large-leaved and smooth-leaved houseplants like dracaena, philodendron, and ficus |
| ○ | ○ | ○ | ○ | ○ | Inspect houseplants for insect pests. Remove insects by hand and spray with insecticidal soap as necessary |
| ○ | ○ | ○ | ○ | ○ | Clean clay pots by soaking overnight in a solution of water and vinegar |

20___

20___

20___

20___

20__

20___

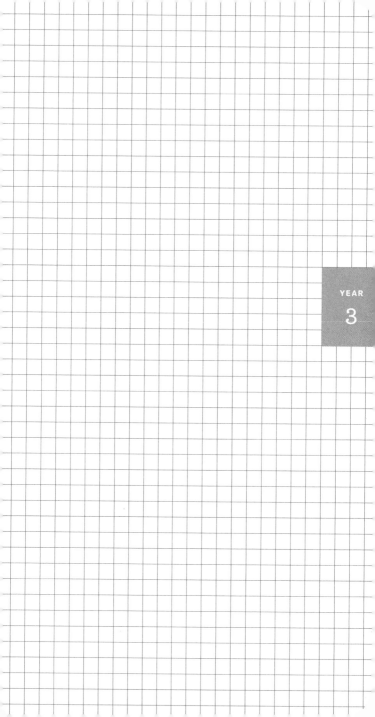

YEAR
3

20__

20___

YEAR
4

20___

20___

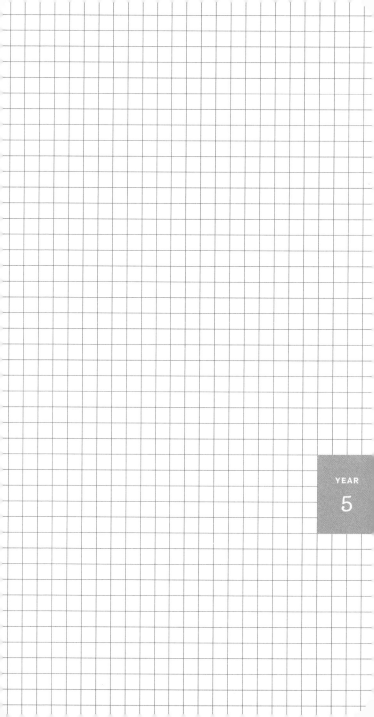

YEAR
5

SPRING

**YEAR**

| 1 | 2 | 3 | 4 | 5 | |
|---|---|---|---|---|---|
| | | | | | *Planning* |
| ○ | ○ | ○ | ○ | ○ | Choose planting areas based on exposure to sun, shade, and wind; consider distance from water source |
| ○ | ○ | ○ | ○ | ○ | Test soil for pH and type before initiating major planting |
| ○ | ○ | ○ | ○ | ○ | Study the garden for gaps that can be filled by spring flowering bulbs and make a list for ordering in late summer for best selection |
| ○ | ○ | ○ | ○ | ○ | Choose flowering trees and shrubs for color and time of bloom to add to the garden when weather conditions permit |
| | | | | | *Chores and Maintenance* |
| ○ | ○ | ○ | ○ | ○ | Carefully remove winter mulches and debris from planting beds |
| ○ | ○ | ○ | ○ | ○ | Dig beds and remove weeds in preparation for spring planting as soon as earth is friable |
| ○ | ○ | ○ | ○ | ○ | Add compost in 2- to 4-inch layers and work into planting bed soil |
| ○ | ○ | ○ | ○ | ○ | Remove protective cover from evergreens |
| ○ | ○ | ○ | ○ | ○ | Reset frost-heaved plants |
| ○ | ○ | ○ | ○ | ○ | Apply horticultural-oil spray to dormant trees and shrubs before buds open and if there is no danger of night frost |
| ○ | ○ | ○ | ○ | ○ | As ground becomes workable, dethatch lawn, aerate and spread compost; fill in low spots with soil; fertilize established lawn |
| ○ | ○ | ○ | ○ | ○ | Place peony supports |
| ○ | ○ | ○ | ○ | ○ | Remove mounded earth from roses |
| ○ | ○ | ○ | ○ | ○ | Prepare bare-root and potted roses for planting by soaking overnight in water |
| ○ | ○ | ○ | ○ | ○ | Test lawn soil and apply lime if warranted |
| ○ | ○ | ○ | ○ | ○ | Dig and divide early-blooming perennials after flowering |

**YEAR**

| 1 | 2 | 3 | 4 | 5 | |
|---|---|---|---|---|---|
| ○ | ○ | ○ | ○ | ○ | Lift, divide, and replant late summer- and fall-blooming perennials |
| ○ | ○ | ○ | ○ | ○ | Set supports for floppy plants, vines, and vegetables |
| ○ | ○ | ○ | ○ | ○ | As grass begins to grow, mow lawns regularly to keep grass at 2½ inches high |
| ○ | ○ | ○ | ○ | ○ | Begin watering program as necessary |
| ○ | ○ | ○ | ○ | ○ | Begin weeding |
| ○ | ○ | ○ | ○ | ○ | Aerate and moisten compost pile to speed decomposition |
| ○ | ○ | ○ | ○ | ○ | Mulch azaleas, rhododendrons, and other ericaceous ornamentals with acid mulch |
| ○ | ○ | ○ | ○ | ○ | Mulch planting beds once soil warms |
| ○ | ○ | ○ | ○ | ○ | Deadhead bulbs but allow foliage to remain until yellow to nourish bulbs for next year's display |
| ○ | ○ | ○ | ○ | ○ | As night temperatures moderate into the 60s, move houseplants outdoors (avoid full sun and windy locations) |
| ○ | ○ | ○ | ○ | ○ | Look for pests and other problems; spotting early can mean less need for chemical controls. Note: slugs and caterpillars can be removed manually |
| ○ | ○ | ○ | ○ | ○ | Begin application of deer repellents |
| | | *Planting* | | | |
| ○ | ○ | ○ | ○ | ○ | Plant deciduous and evergreen trees and shrubs, weather and soil conditions permitting |
| ○ | ○ | ○ | ○ | ○ | Sow seeds indoors of annuals and vegetables that require a later start before transplanting |
| ○ | ○ | ○ | ○ | ○ | Sow radish and lettuce seeds directly into the vegetable garden when temperature allows |

**YEAR**

| 1 | 2 | 3 | 4 | 5 | |
|---|---|---|---|---|---|
| ◯ | ◯ | ◯ | ◯ | ◯ | Plant cold-weather vegetables like spinach, lettuce, and broccoli as soon as soil is workable |
| ◯ | ◯ | ◯ | ◯ | ◯ | Plant and transplant perennials and roses |
| ◯ | ◯ | ◯ | ◯ | ◯ | Soak mail-order bare-root plants before planting |
| ◯ | ◯ | ◯ | ◯ | ◯ | Plant out seedlings of cauliflower, cabbage, and broccoli if soil is workable |
| ◯ | ◯ | ◯ | ◯ | ◯ | Plant out seedlings of cool-season annuals, like pansies and snapdragons |
| ◯ | ◯ | ◯ | ◯ | ◯ | Plant strawberries |
| ◯ | ◯ | ◯ | ◯ | ◯ | Reseed bare lawn areas |
| ◯ | ◯ | ◯ | ◯ | ◯ | Move self-sown annuals and perennials to desired locations |
| ◯ | ◯ | ◯ | ◯ | ◯ | Sow seeds of corn, cucumber, and melon directly in the garden |
| ◯ | ◯ | ◯ | ◯ | ◯ | Harden off tomato, eggplant, and pepper transplants before planting out when weather allows |
| ◯ | ◯ | ◯ | ◯ | ◯ | Plant summer annuals after last frost date (last date that your area might have a killing frost) |
| ◯ | ◯ | ◯ | ◯ | ◯ | Plant summer-flowering bulbs, such as gladiolus and dahlias, after last frost date |
| ◯ | ◯ | ◯ | ◯ | ◯ | Plant caladium and tuberous begonias in shady spots |

*Pruning and Fertilizing*

| 1 | 2 | 3 | 4 | 5 | |
|---|---|---|---|---|---|
| ◯ | ◯ | ◯ | ◯ | ◯ | Prune all plant materials to remove any diseased, dead, weak, or crossing branches |
| ◯ | ◯ | ◯ | ◯ | ◯ | Complete tree pruning before new growth begins |
| ◯ | ◯ | ◯ | ◯ | ◯ | Prune late-flowering shrubs, such as buddleia and *Hydrangea paniculata*, but wait until after flowering on early-flowering shrubs such as forsythia, *Hydrangea macrophylla*, rhododendron, and syringa |

**YEAR**

| 1 | 2 | 3 | 4 | 5 | |
|---|---|---|---|---|---|
| ○ | ○ | ○ | ○ | ○ | Prune all fruit trees before growth begins |
| ○ | ○ | ○ | ○ | ○ | Prune early spring–flowering shrubs immediately after flowers die |
| ○ | ○ | ○ | ○ | ○ | Pinch back late summer- and fall-blooming perennials, such as asters and chrysanthemums once growth accelerates |
| ○ | ○ | ○ | ○ | ○ | Deadhead early roses after blooming |
| ○ | ○ | ○ | ○ | ○ | Cut back ornamental grasses to new shoots as season's growth begins |
| ○ | ○ | ○ | ○ | ○ | Fertilize deciduous broad-leaved evergreens if not fed in the fall |
| ○ | ○ | ○ | ○ | ○ | Fertilize and lime vegetable garden |
| ○ | ○ | ○ | ○ | ○ | Fertilize fruit trees and roses |
| ○ | ○ | ○ | ○ | ○ | Fertilize perennials when you see 2 to 3 inches of new growth |
| ○ | ○ | ○ | ○ | ○ | Fertilize bulbs as they finish blooming |
| ○ | ○ | ○ | ○ | ○ | Fertilize needle-leaved evergreens with acid-type fertilizer |
| ○ | ○ | ○ | ○ | ○ | Fertilize annuals and container plants, monthly, or use slow-release fertilizer |
| ○ | ○ | ○ | ○ | ○ | Fertilize lawns in late May |
| | | | | | *Indoors* |
| ○ | ○ | ○ | ○ | ○ | Begin to transplant pot-bound houseplants |
| ○ | ○ | ○ | ○ | ○ | Cut back leggy houseplants |
| ○ | ○ | ○ | ○ | ○ | Take houseplants outside as temperatures moderate; move to partially shaded, wind-protected location |

20___

20___

20__

20___

_____

_____

_____

_____

_____

_____

_____

_____

_____

_____

_____

_____

_____

_____

_____

_____

_____

_____

_____

_____

_____

_____

_____

_____

_____

_____

20__

20____

YEAR

3

20__

20___

20___

20___

SUMMER

**YEAR**

1  2  3  4  5

## Planning

| 1 | 2 | 3 | 4 | 5 | |
|---|---|---|---|---|---|
| ○ | ○ | ○ | ○ | ○ | Order spring-flowering bulbs for fall planting |
| ○ | ○ | ○ | ○ | ○ | Assess areas in the garden that may need new or replacement planting |
| ○ | ○ | ○ | ○ | ○ | Prepare a landscape plan for fall planting of trees and shrubs |
| ○ | ○ | ○ | ○ | ○ | Continue to take garden notes and/or photographs to plan future plantings |

## Chores and Maintenance

| 1 | 2 | 3 | 4 | 5 | |
|---|---|---|---|---|---|
| ○ | ○ | ○ | ○ | ○ | Deadhead rhododendrons, lilacs, and perennials after flowering |
| ○ | ○ | ○ | ○ | ○ | Add to, aerate, and moisten compost pile to speed decomposition |
| ○ | ○ | ○ | ○ | ○ | Water lawns if there is less than 1 inch of rain per week |
| ○ | ○ | ○ | ○ | ○ | Spray roses every week with baking soda solution to protect against black spot disease (Cornell University's formula consists of 3 teaspoons baking soda and 2½ tablespoons summer-weight horticultural oil, mixed with 1 gallon of water) |
| ○ | ○ | ○ | ○ | ○ | If the weather has been dry, practice water-wise horticultural techniques |
| ○ | ○ | ○ | ○ | ○ | Determine which plants are most important and water them first |
| ○ | ○ | ○ | ○ | ○ | Water plants early in the day through drip irrigation or hand-held hose with shut-off nozzle |
| ○ | ○ | ○ | ○ | ○ | Reapply mulch to help conserve moisture |
| ○ | ○ | ○ | ○ | ○ | Allow lawns to go dormant; they will green up again when rain returns |
| ○ | ○ | ○ | ○ | ○ | Continue to remove weeds, which compete for water |
| ○ | ○ | ○ | ○ | ○ | Continue to stake floppy plants and vines |

**YEAR**

| 1 | 2 | 3 | 4 | 5 | |
|---|---|---|---|---|---|
| ○ | ○ | ○ | ○ | ○ | Mow lawns regularly to keep grass 2 to 2½ inches high |
| ○ | ○ | ○ | ○ | ○ | Apply acid mulch to rhododendrons, azaleas, and other ericaceous ornamentals |
| ○ | ○ | ○ | ○ | ○ | Apply a summer mulch to rose beds to preserve moisture and control weeds |
| ○ | ○ | ○ | ○ | ○ | Deadhead annuals and perennials to encourage continuous bloom, and cut back any rampant growth |
| ○ | ○ | ○ | ○ | ○ | Spot-seed to renovate existing lawn between mid-August and mid-September |
| ○ | ○ | ○ | ○ | ○ | Check for insect pests and treat accordingly |
| ○ | ○ | ○ | ○ | ○ | Remove any fallen leaves and debris, which can harbor insect pests and disease organisms |
| ○ | ○ | ○ | ○ | ○ | Continue to apply deer repellent |
| ○ | ○ | ○ | ○ | ○ | Cut flowers such as yarrow, strawflower, gomphrena, and cockscomb for drying |

*Planting*

| 1 | 2 | 3 | 4 | 5 | |
|---|---|---|---|---|---|
| ○ | ○ | ○ | ○ | ○ | Complete moving self-sown annuals and perennials to desired locations |
| ○ | ○ | ○ | ○ | ○ | Sow seeds of fast-growing annuals like marigolds, zinnias, and cosmos directly in the garden |
| ○ | ○ | ○ | ○ | ○ | Sow seeds of heat-tolerant vegetables |
| ○ | ○ | ○ | ○ | ○ | Finish planting summer annuals |
| ○ | ○ | ○ | ○ | ○ | Finish planting summer-flowering bulbs, corms, and tubers, such as cannas, gladiolus, and dahlias in early summer |
| ○ | ○ | ○ | ○ | ○ | Plant caladium and tuberous begonias in shady spots |
| ○ | ○ | ○ | ○ | ○ | In late summer, sow seed of lettuce, kale, broccoli, cabbage, radishes, beets, carrots, turnips, and arugula for fall harvest |

**YEAR**

| 1 | 2 | 3 | 4 | 5 | |
|---|---|---|---|---|---|
| ○ | ○ | ○ | ○ | ○ | In late summer, sow seeds of cool-weather annuals |
| ○ | ○ | ○ | ○ | ○ | Propagate spring-flowering perennials |
| ○ | ○ | ○ | ○ | ○ | Propagate herbs from new growth and transplant into pots for winter use as days get colder |
| ○ | ○ | ○ | ○ | ○ | Divide bearded iris after flowering and dispose of any borer-damaged parts |
| ○ | ○ | ○ | ○ | ○ | Plant late-season annuals like ornamental kale and cabbage for fall color |
| ○ | ○ | ○ | ○ | ○ | In late summer, plant out seedlings of cool-weather vegetable plants for fall harvest |
| ○ | ○ | ○ | ○ | ○ | Plant out seedling biennials for next year's bloom |
| ○ | ○ | ○ | ○ | ○ | Plant broad-leaved and needle-leaved evergreens from late August through October 15 |

### Pruning and Fertilizing

| 1 | 2 | 3 | 4 | 5 | |
|---|---|---|---|---|---|
| ○ | ○ | ○ | ○ | ○ | Continue pruning all plant material to remove any diseased, dead, weak, or crossing branches |
| ○ | ○ | ○ | ○ | ○ | Prune evergreens and evergreen hedges into early summer |
| ○ | ○ | ○ | ○ | ○ | Deadhead hybrid tea, floribunda, grandiflora, miniature, repeat-blooming, shrub, and climbing roses |
| ○ | ○ | ○ | ○ | ○ | Prune and thin large shade trees to increase light for lawns and planting beds |
| ○ | ○ | ○ | ○ | ○ | Prune to the ground all raspberry canes that have completed fruiting |
| ○ | ○ | ○ | ○ | ○ | Lightly prune overgrown hedges and deciduous shrubs |
| ○ | ○ | ○ | ○ | ○ | Prune summer-flowering trees and shrubs once flowering is complete |
| ○ | ○ | ○ | ○ | ○ | Cut back leggy annuals |

**YEAR**

| 1 | 2 | 3 | 4 | 5 | |
|---|---|---|---|---|---|
| ○ | ○ | ○ | ○ | ○ | Feed broad-leaved and needle-leaved evergreens with iron chelate if leaves are yellowing |
| ○ | ○ | ○ | ○ | ○ | Fertilize roses to encourage last new growth and harden off before frost |
| ○ | ○ | ○ | ○ | ○ | Continue to fertilize annuals and container plants each month |
| ○ | ○ | ○ | ○ | ○ | Fertilize broad-leaved flowering evergreen shrubs with topdressing of oak-leaf compost and/or cottonseed meal |
| ○ | ○ | ○ | ○ | ○ | Fertilize needle-leaved evergreens with acid-type fertilizer |
| ○ | ○ | ○ | ○ | ○ | Fertilize chrysanthemums every two to three weeks until buds form, then fertilize weekly until buds show color |
| ○ | ○ | ○ | ○ | ○ | Fertilize vegetables |

*Indoors*

| 1 | 2 | 3 | 4 | 5 | |
|---|---|---|---|---|---|
| ○ | ○ | ○ | ○ | ○ | Shape and pinch back houseplants before returning them indoors as temperatures drop |
| ○ | ○ | ○ | ○ | ○ | Check houseplants for insect pests and treat as necessary before bringing them in |

20___

20___

20__

20__

20___

20___

20___

20___

20___

20__

FALL

**YEAR**

| 1 | 2 | 3 | 4 | 5 | |
|---|---|---|---|---|---|
| | | | | | *Planning* |
| ○ | ○ | ○ | ○ | ○ | Complete orders of spring-flowering bulbs and other plants for fall planting |
| ○ | ○ | ○ | ○ | ○ | Assess areas in the garden that may need new or replacement planting |
| ○ | ○ | ○ | ○ | ○ | Work on your landscape plan for fall planting of trees and shrubs |
| ○ | ○ | ○ | ○ | ○ | Take garden notes and photos to plan future planting |
| ○ | ○ | ○ | ○ | ○ | Prepare landscape sketches for next growing season |
| ○ | ○ | ○ | ○ | ○ | Have soil tested at local Cooperative Extension Service to determine pH and nutritional levels |
| | | | | | *Chores and Maintenance* |
| ○ | ○ | ○ | ○ | ○ | If it is dry, practice water-wise horticultural techniques |
| ○ | ○ | ○ | ○ | ○ | Dethatch and aerate lawns to promote root growth |
| ○ | ○ | ○ | ○ | ○ | Mow lawns regularly to keep grass 2½ to 3 inches high |
| ○ | ○ | ○ | ○ | ○ | Complete spot seeding and lawn restoration by September 15 |
| ○ | ○ | ○ | ○ | ○ | Collect seed from perennials and annuals |
| ○ | ○ | ○ | ○ | ○ | Remove and compost spent annuals |
| ○ | ○ | ○ | ○ | ○ | Aerate and moisten compost pile to speed decomposition |
| ○ | ○ | ○ | ○ | ○ | Check for insect pests and treat accordingly |
| ○ | ○ | ○ | ○ | ○ | Remove fallen leaves and debris that can harbor insect pests and disease |
| ○ | ○ | ○ | ○ | ○ | Apply deer repellent |
| ○ | ○ | ○ | ○ | ○ | If it is dry, continue to thoroughly water trees, shrubs, planting beds, and lawn areas, especially evergreen plantings |
| ○ | ○ | ○ | ○ | ○ | Continue to weed, weed, weed |

**YEAR**

| 1 | 2 | 3 | 4 | 5 | |
|---|---|---|---|---|---|
| ○ | ○ | ○ | ○ | ○ | Stake chrysanthemums, water, and fertilize |
| ○ | ○ | ○ | ○ | ○ | Lift and store tender bulbs, corms, and tubers, such as cannas, dahlias, and gladiolus, after first frost |
| ○ | ○ | ○ | ○ | ○ | Complete removal of fallen leaves and debris to protect from overwintering of insects and disease organisms |
| ○ | ○ | ○ | ○ | ○ | Cut back perennials to 4 to 5 inches, but leave ornamental grasses to provide winter interest until spring |
| ○ | ○ | ○ | ○ | ○ | Mulch boxwood and broad-leaved evergreens before ground freezes |
| ○ | ○ | ○ | ○ | ○ | Mulch flower beds to keep ground temperature stable and prevent winter injury from frost heaving |
| ○ | ○ | ○ | ○ | ○ | Provide burlap windbreaks for boxwood and broad-leaved evergreens; install stakes before ground freezes |
| ○ | ○ | ○ | ○ | ○ | Protect trees from mouse damage with wire-mesh trunk guards |
| ○ | ○ | ○ | ○ | ○ | Protect shrubs from deer with burlap or netting |
| ○ | ○ | ○ | ○ | ○ | Mow lawn one final time to 1½ to 2 inches high |
| ○ | ○ | ○ | ○ | ○ | Aerate soil around rose roots and hill up earth 10 to 12 inches around the crowns after a heavy frost |

*Planting*

| 1 | 2 | 3 | 4 | 5 | |
|---|---|---|---|---|---|
| ○ | ○ | ○ | ○ | ○ | Plant and transplant broad-leaved and needle-leaved evergreens through October 15 |
| ○ | ○ | ○ | ○ | ○ | Propagate herbs from new growth and transplant into pots for winter use |
| ○ | ○ | ○ | ○ | ○ | Continue to divide and transplant early-blooming perennials |
| ○ | ○ | ○ | ○ | ○ | Divide daylilies after flowering |
| ○ | ○ | ○ | ○ | ○ | Plant lilies |

**YEAR**

| 1 | 2 | 3 | 4 | 5 | |
|---|---|---|---|---|---|
| ○ | ○ | ○ | ○ | ○ | If weather turns cool, begin planting spring-flowering bulbs (wait until late October for tulips) |
| ○ | ○ | ○ | ○ | ○ | Plant late-season ornamentals, like ornamental kale and cabbage, for fall color |
| ○ | ○ | ○ | ○ | ○ | Plant out seeding biennials |
| ○ | ○ | ○ | ○ | ○ | Plant and transplant deciduous trees and shrubs after leaf fall and before ground freezes |
| ○ | ○ | ○ | ○ | ○ | Plant spinach and garlic |
| ○ | ○ | ○ | ○ | ○ | Complete lifting and dividing irises, lilies of the valley, and daylilies |
| ○ | ○ | ○ | ○ | ○ | Plant bare-root roses |
| ○ | ○ | ○ | ○ | ○ | Pot up amaryllis, tulip, and other prepared bulbs and store in a cool, dark place until ready to force for indoor blooms |
| ○ | ○ | ○ | ○ | ○ | Propagate deciduous shrubs, such as hydrangea, viburnum, and weigela; and evergreen shrubs, such as holly, juniper, and yew |

### Pruning and Fertilizing

| 1 | 2 | 3 | 4 | 5 | |
|---|---|---|---|---|---|
| ○ | ○ | ○ | ○ | ○ | Prune rambling roses |
| ○ | ○ | ○ | ○ | ○ | Remove diseased and dead rose canes |
| ○ | ○ | ○ | ○ | ○ | Root-prune wisteria that doesn't bloom |
| ○ | ○ | ○ | ○ | ○ | Add organic matter, such as manure, compost, and/or leaf mold, to improve garden soil |
| ○ | ○ | ○ | ○ | ○ | Prune late-blooming trees and shrubs once dormant |
| ○ | ○ | ○ | ○ | ○ | If needed, prune early spring–flowering shrubs to remove diseased and damaged branches but preserve buds |
| ○ | ○ | ○ | ○ | ○ | Fertilize roses one last time |

**YEAR**

1 2 3 4 5

| | | | | | |
|---|---|---|---|---|---|
| ○ | ○ | ○ | ○ | ○ | Fertilize lawns with organic fertilizer to stimulate winter root development |
| ○ | ○ | ○ | ○ | ○ | Fertilize trees and shrubs before ground freezes so they have food in early spring |
| ○ | ○ | ○ | ○ | ○ | Incorporate lime and fertilizer in the annual and vegetable gardens for next growing season |

*Indoors*

| | | | | | |
|---|---|---|---|---|---|
| ○ | ○ | ○ | ○ | ○ | If frost threatens, pinch back houseplants and treat for insect pests as necessary before bringing indoors |
| ○ | ○ | ○ | ○ | ○ | Begin to force poinsettias for holiday display; move indoors to a sunny location and cover for fourteen hours each night for six to ten weeks |
| ○ | ○ | ○ | ○ | ○ | Take cuttings of begonias, geraniums, coleus, and others to grow as houseplants |
| ○ | ○ | ○ | ○ | ○ | Give houseplants as much light as possible as lower-light days begin |
| ○ | ○ | ○ | ○ | ○ | Provide houseplants with increased humidity; mist often or place the plants over a tray of moist pebbles |
| ○ | ○ | ○ | ○ | ○ | Pot up prepared bulbs for indoor forcing |
| ○ | ○ | ○ | ○ | ○ | Begin to increase the time between waterings, but water thoroughly each time |

20___

20___

20___

20___

FALL

20___

20___

20___

20___

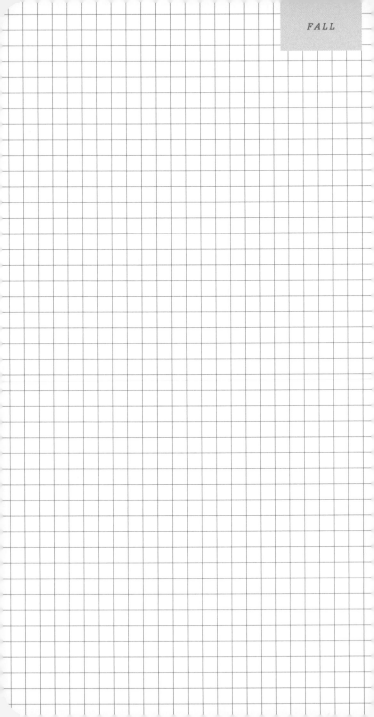

20___

20___

_____

Plants need good soil to thrive. Soil not only anchors a plant but supplies nutrients, water, and oxygen. Healthy soil means healthy plants; plants grown in fertile soil are less prone to pest and disease problems.

You can improve your garden's soil by adding compost to it. Often called "black gold," compost is rich in humus, decaying organic matter that conditions the soil structure and benefits drainage, aeration, texture, moisture retention, and ability to hold nutrients, which are taken up through the roots as needed by the plant. (Nutrients include nitrogen, phosphorus, potassium, and essential trace elements.)

Making your own compost is easy to do, once you understand the method. You can make compost in your backyard using decomposable kitchen waste and refuse from the garden in as little as four to six weeks, but it usually takes three to six months, more frequently a year, depending on the holding unit used. Compost is made by digging, layering, turning, and watering the heap. The transformation is accomplished by decomposer living organisms.

Ingredients for compost fall into two categories, browns and greens. The ideal brown (carbon) to green (nitrogen) ratio is 20:1 or 30:1.

» *Browns are dry materials such as straw, dried leaves, dried grass clippings, wood chips, sawdust, and refuse from pruning. You can also use paper bags, newspapers (though these may contain heavy metals), egg cartons, milk cartons, and cereal boxes—as long as they're clean, dry, and well shredded.*

---

» *Greens are moist, fresh food scraps (like vegetable peels, eggshells, fruit rinds, coffee and tea grounds, and nutshells) and refuse from the garden—recent lawn clippings, weeds, stalks, almost anything organic except dense wood.*

» *Do not use fatty meats and bones, pet waste, oil or grease, dairy products, diseased plants, or weeds that have gone to seed.*

» *Material that is 1/2 to 1 1/2 inches in size breaks down best. Any hard or woody material should be chopped up, shredded, or run through a lawn mower.*

The best-composed finished compost product contains a diversity of materials. For instance, consider adding alfalfa (provides nitrogen), beet tops (provide calcium, magnesium, nitrogen), citrus rinds (provide potash), coffee grounds and filters (provide nitrogen, are acidic, preserve moisture, and deodorize compost heap), peanut shells (provide potassium), and soil (provides minerals and microorganisms, among other things).

You can make compost in a pile or trench in your backyard (in the shade, to retain needed moisture), use a large plastic garbage container perforated on the sides and bottom for aeration and drainage, construct a crib out of wire mesh, or purchase a composting bin. For a backyard pile, a good size is 3 to 4 feet square and 3 feet high; anything smaller will not hold moisture well or have enough volume to retain the heat that fosters rapid decomposition.

For the foundation layer of the pile, choose coarse material like stalks or hay. Next, alternate equal layers of brown and green materials, wetting each with water. Finally, soak the pile until it is uniformly moist and about as damp as a wrung-out sponge. Cover with a tarp to keep moisture in and prevent it from getting too wet if it rains.

Water the compost pile regularly to keep the consistency continually spongy but not soggy. Turn the pile at least once a week to move outside material to the center and aerate the contents. Once a pile is started, don't add new materials or you will slow down the process because organic matter needs time to decompose.

When the compost pile begins to generate steam, you'll know that the matter is breaking down. As the pile decomposes, its temperature will rise. The pile should heat up to about 150°F in its center over about four days and then gradually cool after a week or two. When the pile is decomposing rapidly, it will give off a relatively pleasant odor, generate heat and steam, lose volume, and become dark brown. You can accelerate the process by turning the pile every other day, or mixing in manure of vegetable-eating animals or commercial compost activators.

As composting nears completion, the temperature drops until little heat is produced. Look for dark, rich brown material that is fully decomposed and has no traces of food waste. Although compost is then ready to use, let it cure for up to two weeks. Once the compost is ready, mix it into seedbeds and garden soil, and spread it as topdressing on lawns, using ½ to 1 pound per square foot.

## FOR MORE INFORMATION

### WEBSITES AND ARTICLES

**Ten Steps to Making Thermal Compost, Soil Foodweb Inc.**
soilfoodweb.com/Thermal_Compost.html

**Soil and Composting: Soil Improvement, eXtension**
articles.extension.org/pages/13048/soils-and-composting:-soil-improvement#.VE-vBfnrzA8

**Home Composting and Reducing Wasted Food, New York State Department of Environmental Conservation**
dec.ny.gov/chemical/8799.html

Information on composting, workshops, demonstrations, and a
certificate program offered by the New York City Compost Project in
the Bronx

nybg.org/gardens/bronx-green-up/nyc-compost-project/

libguides.nybg.org/compostdays?hs=a

**The Compost Tea Brewing Manual, Soil Foodweb Inc.**
ecologiesurleweb.free.fr/docs/Docs_agir/Lombricomposteur/
Brew%20Manual%20compost%20tea.pdf

**Compost Teas and Extracts, Permaculture News**
permaculturenews.org/2012/07/11/compost-teas-and-extracts-
brewin-and-bubblin-basics/

## BOOKS

**Dunne, Niall, ed.** *Healthy Soils for Sustainable Gardens.* Brooklyn, NY:
Brooklyn Botanic Garden, 2009.

**Hanson, Beth, and Niall Dunne, eds.** *Easy Compost.* Brooklyn, NY:
Brooklyn Botanic Garden, 2013.

**Lowenfels, Jeff, and Wayne Lewis.** *Teaming with Microbes: The
Organic Gardener's Guide to the Soil Food Web.* Portland, OR:
Timber Press, 2010.

**Ondra, Nancy J.** *Soil and Composting.* Taylor's Weekend Gardening
Guides. Boston: Houghton Mifflin, 1998.

# CONTAINER GARDENING

Container gardens are great ways to create a garden when you don't have a yard. They are easy to use and versatile, and come in a wide variety of shapes and sizes.

## CONTAINER BASICS

» *Use containers with holes in the bottom for drainage.*

» *Larger containers require less frequent watering.*

» *Add Styrofoam peanuts, old plastic pots (overturned), or any light material to the bases of large containers so that they do not become too heavy to move.*

» *Use potting soil in your containers. Garden soil is too heavy and may not be free from pests and diseases.*

» *Space the plants much closer than you would in the garden— in containers, you can grow twice as many plants in the same amount of space.*

» *Don't fill the containers to the top with soil and mulch. Leave 1 to 2 inches at the top to allow for easier watering and to keep soil and mulch from spilling out.*

» *Fertilize your containers. Nutrients will leach out with frequent watering. Use half the amount of fertilizer recommended on the label; overfertilizing weakens plants and promotes leafy growth with few flowers.*

» *Deadhead your flowers regularly to keep them blooming. Cut back or prune any plants that become too large.*

» *Check containers daily to see if they need to be watered.*

## DESIGN CONSIDERATIONS

» **FOLIAGE** *is an important and often underrated component of any design, whether in a container or in the garden. Long after flowers are gone, foliage continues to provide wonderful contrasts and textures.*

» **TEXTURES** *that are feathery and delicate enhance foliage and colors in neighboring plants. Bold textures create an impact, adding stability to a design and creating focal points.*

» **SHAPES** *of plants have various functions. Container designers categorize plants into three types by their shape and function: accent plants, fillers, and trailing plants. Accent plants have striking features that create a focal point for the composition; examples include vertical plants that give the container height and tropical plants, with their broad leaves and exotic feel. Fillers add mass and color to an arrangement. Mounding plants are wonderful fillers. Trailing plants spill over the edge of the pot or basket and blur the lines between container and plant. They are important features of hanging baskets.*

» **COLORS** *may be hot (red, orange, and yellow) or cool (blue, purple, and pink). White often brings out the intensity in another color, looking very elegant when paired with green, and pastel and pretty when paired with pale yellow. Beautiful arrangements can be made by combining varying shades or hues of the same color.*

» **REPETITION** *creates continuity in an arrangement and ties the composition together. With too much variety, the eye does not have a resting point. Repetition can mean using the same plant throughout a grouping of containers, using plants with the same color or shape, or using the same plant in different colors.*

» **SCALE AND PROPORTION** *are important considerations. Layer contrasting heights in tiers from tall to small; large accent plants can dwarf the other plants in a container unless there are transitional, medium-height plants to draw the eye to the underplanting. Layering also covers up the bare undergrowth of taller plants. Tall plants look best in pots with wide bases, and small, rounded containers look best when planted with mounding plants that mimic the shape of the container.*

» **CREATING MINIATURE LANDSCAPES** *is attractive. Group a number of containers together to establish a tableau. Plants with contrasting shapes or textures can be placed side by side very effectively. Many plants thrive when planted separately, rather than competing for space in a crowded container. Grasses, for instance, look wonderful when given center stage in a pot all by themselves.*

## FOR MORE INFORMATION

### WEBSITES

**NYBG Container Gardening: Pots Galore!**
libguides.nybg.org/containergardening?hs=a

**Container Gardening in Drought**
**Drought-Resistant Plants for Pots, Brooklyn Botanic Garden**
bbg.org/gardening/article/drought-resistant_plants_for_pots

**Successful Container Gardens, University of Illinois Extension**
extension.illinois.edu/containergardening/

### BOOKS

**Appell, Scott D.** *The Potted Garden: New Plants and New Approaches for Container Gardens.* Brooklyn, NY: Brooklyn Botanic Garden, 2001.

**Eddison, Sydney.** *Gardens to Go: Creating and Designing a Container Garden.* New York: Bulfinch Press, 2005.

**Guerra, Michael.** *The Edible Container Garden: Growing Fresh Food in Small Spaces.* New York: Fireside, 2000.

**Joyce, David.** *The Complete Container Garden.* Pleasantville, NY: Reader's Digest, 2003.

# PRUNING BASICS

Pruning promotes plant health; improves the size and appearance of plants, shrubs, and trees; and encourages more or larger fruits and flowers. Thinning out lets more light into the center of the plant and improves air circulation around the plant, making it less susceptible to pests and diseases. Pruning rejuvenates old plants, restoring their vigor.

Use sturdy, safe, well-made pruning tools with sharp blades, and be sure you have the right tool for each pruning job. Keep your tools clean, sharp, and ready to use. Most tools can be easily cleaned by wiping them with a rag after use or cleaning with WD-40. Sharpen blades with a file or take tools to your local garden center for care. If you cut diseased wood, clean your tools with rubbing alcohol to avoid spreading the disease. Basic pruning tools include

» *Bypass pruners*

» *Lopping shears or loppers*

» *Pruning saws*

» *Hedge shears*

Plants respond differently to pruning depending on the plant and on how you make your cut.

» *Simply pinching out the top growing point of a plant slows down the top growth and induces side shoots to grow, producing bushier plants.*

» *A heading cut shortens a stem. As with pinching, the cut will stimulate side shoots to grow. A small cut encourages many new buds on the stem to grow; a larger cut produces fewer yet larger side shoots.*

» *To thin a plant, remove a branch in its entirety. This prevents any regrowth.*

When to prune depends on your climate and the plant. Consult the New York Botanical Garden website or your county cooperative extension office for information on individual plants in your hardiness zone. As a general rule, plants that flower early in spring or flower on old wood (previous season's growth) should be pruned immediately after they flower. Plants that flower on new wood (current season's growth) should be pruned in late winter or early spring.

Before pruning, consider the natural shape of a tree or shrub so that you can work with it to make it look its best. Start by choosing the right plant for the right place and knowing the plant's mature size before you introduce it into your landscape.

Here's how to cut:

» *Cut above a bud (at least ¼ inch above).*

» *Cut at an angle away from the bud (generally a 45-degree angle) to ensure that water runs off the cut and doesn't rot the new bud.*

» *When removing a larger branch (more than 1½ inches), follow the three-cut rule to avoid tearing the bark. Make the first cut underneath the branch, a foot or two from the trunk, cutting through one quarter of the wood. Next, cut off the branch several inches farther from the trunk, cutting from above. Finally, cut off the remaining stub, making sure not to cut into the branch collar, where the stem adjoins the trunk.*

When pruning a shrub, take off no more than one-third of the material; for trees, no more than one-fourth of the live foliage. Remove only dead and diseased wood the first year and begin pruning after the plant has become established. Many trees and shrubs need little pruning—just an occasional shaping and cleaning out of dead material.

Rejuvenate old shrubs by removing one-third of the old wood each year over the course of three years. If an old shrub is damaged or you want to give it one last chance, cut the majority of the shrub back hard (to within 1 to 2 feet), leaving at least two branches intact with foliage, so the shrub can photosynthesize. This should be done just before bud-break to induce maximum growth.

## FOR MORE INFORMATION

### WEBSITES AND ARTICLES

**NYBG Pruning: An Introduction**
libguides.nybg.org/pruningintro?hs=a

**Fruit Trees: Training and Pruning Deciduous Trees, University of California, Division of Agriculture and Natural Resources**
homeorchard.ucdavis.edu/8057.pdf

**Our Rose Garden: Pruning, University of Illinois Extension**
extension.illinois.edu/roses/prune.cfm

**Training and Pruning Fruit Trees, Colorado State University Extension**
extension.colostate.edu/topic-areas/yard-garden/training-and-pruning-fruit-trees-7-003/

**A Guide to Successful Pruning, Pruning Shrubs, Virginia Cooperative Extension**
pubs.ext.vt.edu/430/430-459/430-459.html

## BOOKS

**Brown, George E., and Tony Kirkham.** *The Pruning of Trees, Shrubs, and Conifers,* Second edition. Portland, OR: Timber Press, 2009.

**Cutler, Karan Davis.** *Pruning Trees, Shrubs, and Vines.* Brooklyn, NY: Brooklyn Botanic Garden, 2003.

**Gilman, Edward F.** *An Illustrated Guide to Pruning,* Third edition. Clifton Park, NY: Delmar, 2012.

**Hill, Lewis.** *Pruning Made Easy: A Gardener's Visual Guide to When and How to Prune Everything, from Flowers to Trees.* Pownal, VT: Storey, 1997.

**Reich, Lee.** *The Pruning Book,* Second edition. Newtown, CT: Taunton, 2010.

**Turnbull, Cass.** *Cass Turnbull's Guide to Pruning: What, When, Where, and How to Prune for a More Beautiful Garden,* Third edition. Seattle: Sasquatch Books, 2012.

# CONTROLLING PESTS AND DISEASES

Most gardeners today agree that practicing integrated pest management (IPM) is the most environmentally healthy and garden-friendly way to control pests and plant disease. Integrated pest management advocates protecting human and non-target populations by using a minimum of pesticides and instead harnessing control measures that exist naturally. It focuses on following good horticultural practices first and using chemicals in an effective and targeted manner only after other management options have been exhausted. The four kinds of controls pest management integrates are cultural, physical, biological, and chemical.

To manage pests in your garden, try the first three types of controls before turning to chemical methods.

» *Choose, when possible, plants that are native to your region; they are generally more disease- and pest-resistant. Purchase disease-resistant varieties and use certified disease-free seed. Inspect planting stock carefully before buying it.*

» *Analyze site characteristics, including soil, sun, wind paths, and drainage, and select suitable plants. Do not overcrowd; planting too closely will lead to poor air circulation and can result in disease.*

» *Prepare and maintain good soil. Amending soil with compost or well-rotted manure makes plants healthier and more disease-resistant. Mulch to conserve moisture and reduce weeds.*

» *Keep plants well watered in hot weather. Water early in the day, so moisture is available during the hours of sun, and direct the water to the base of the plant, avoiding the foliage. Don't overwater or underwater.*

» Prune away leaves and branches that are dead, diseased, or pest-infested. Move diseased materials away from your garden and destroy them to prevent disease from spreading.

» Use clean tools. Sterilize equipment with household bleach diluted 1:9 with water. Wash hands and clean off shoes.

» Scout for pests weekly, and treat any potential problems with garden-friendly means such as handpicking unwanted insects, spraying off insects with water, and using nontoxic sprays targeted to specific pests and plants. If you detect symptoms of plant disease, deal with the problem immediately.

» In vegetable gardens, use row covers as physical barriers to keep pests from reaching target vegetables, or cover plants with insect netting.

» Try companion planting. Plants with strong fragrances, like marigolds and scented geraniums, confuse many pests and prevent them from finding target hosts.

» Use trap crops to lure pests away from valuable plants. For example, four-o'clocks, scented geraniums, or larkspur planted near roses may act as decoys, attracting Japanese beetles to eat their poisonous leaves.

» Spraying plant leaves with a homemade pepper spray of water, a few drops of hot pepper sauce, and a sprinkle of cayenne pepper may deter aphids, spider mites, whiteflies, leafhoppers, and other soft-bodied insects and even help repel some mammals.

If you detect pest infestation, try biological controls before chemical:

» *Two environmentally friendly insecticides available to gardeners are products that come from naturally occurring bacteria: Bt (Bacillus thuringiensis) and spinosad. Different strains of Bt act against caterpillars, flies, and beetles, while spinosad targets aphids, whiteflies, thrips, leafhoppers, cucumber beetles, and a whole host of pests.*

» *Insecticidal soap and horticultural oil are natural alternatives to chemicals. Always read the label. Use vegetable-based and not petroleum-based oils on vegetable plants.*

» *Nematodes are effective on many pest problems. Some companies, such as BASF, specialize in these beneficial nematode products.*

» *Milky spore (a bacterium), applied to the lawn, causes a lethal disease specific to Japanese beetle grubs.*

» *Natural enemies of garden pests—such as lady beetles, lacewings, and beneficial wasps—provide constant control if enough are present in the landscape. Plants of the daisy family (Asteraceae) and the carrot family (Apiaceae) attract beneficial insects.*

» *Traps can be used to control some insects and animals.*

» *One of the least toxic and most effective controls for the powdery mildew fungus is the Cornell formula. Add 1 tablespoon of baking soda and 1 tablespoon of light vegetable oil or summer-weight horticultural oil to 1 gallon of water. Shake well. Spray both the tops and undersides of all leaves once a week or following a heavy rainstorm.*

» *Allow for a tolerable level of insect damage. Use nonorganic chemical treatments as a last resort.*

**FOR MORE INFORMATION**

## WEBSITES AND ARTICLES

**Regional IPM Centers, U.S. Department of Agriculture**
ipmcenters.org

**Integrated Pest Management, NSF Center for Integrated Pest Management, North Carolina State University**
cipm.info

**Integrated Pest Management, University of California, Integrated Pest Management Program**
ipm.ucanr.edu

**Pest Notes Library, University of California, Division of Agriculture and Natural Resources**
ipm.ucanr.edu/PMG/PESTNOTES/

**Deer Deterrents: Scents, University of Vermont**
uvm.edu/pss/ppp/articles/deerdeter.html

**Deer, Internet Center for Wildlife Damage Management, Cornell University**
icwdm.org/handbook/mammals/Deer.asp

**A Treatise on Squirrelly Pests, Cornell Cooperative Extension, Westchester County**
s3.amazonaws.com/assets.cce.cornell.edu/
attachments/13087/A_Treatise_on_Squirrelly_Pests.
pdf?1453911845

**Hot Pepper Spray, Organic Growers School: Ask Ruth**
organicgrowersschool.org/1927/ask-ruth-hot-pepper-spray/

**Home Vegetable Garden Insect Pest Control, Oklahoma Cooperative Extension Service**
pods.dasnr.okstate.edu/docushare/dsweb/Get/Document-1317/F-7313web.pdf

**Managing Insects in the Home Vegetable Garden, Purdue Extension**
extension.entm.purdue.edu/publications/E-21.pdf

**Pest Control and Pesticide Safety for Consumers, Environmental Protection Agency**
epa.gov/safepestcontrol

**Beneficials in the Garden and Landscape, Galveston County Master Gardeners**
aggie-horticulture.tamu.edu/galveston/beneficials/index.htm

**Weed Identification, New York State Integrated Pest Management, Cornell University**
nysipm.cornell.edu/agriculture/vegetables/weed-identification

## BOOKS

**Agrios, George N.** *Plant Pathology.* Cambridge, MA: Academic Press, 2005.

**Bradley, Fern Marshall, Barbara W. Ellis, and Deborah L. Martin, eds.** *The Organic Gardener's Handbook of Natural Pest and Disease Control: A Complete Guide to Maintaining a Healthy Garden and Yard the Earth-Friendly Way.* New York: Rodale, 2009.

**Deardorff, David, and Kathryn Wadsworth.** *What's Wrong with My Houseplant? Save Your Indoor Plants with 100% Organic Solutions.* Portland, OR: Timber Press, 2016.

**Deardorff, David, and Kathryn Wadsworth.** *What's Wrong with My Vegetable Garden? 100% Organic Solutions for All Your Vegetables, from Artichokes to Zucchini.* Portland, OR: Timber Press, 2011.

**Greenwood, Pippa, A. R. Chase, Daniel Gilrein, and Andrew Halstead.** *American Horticultural Society Pests and Diseases: The Complete Guide to Preventing, Identifying, and Treating Plant Problems.* New York: Dorling Kindersley, 2000.

**Mikolajski, Andrew.** *The Complete Illustrated Book of Garden Pests and Diseases and How to Get Rid of Them.* London: Southwater Publishing, 2009.

**Thomas, Kenneth W., Barbara Ellis, and Frances Tenenbaum, eds.** *Organic Pest and Disease Control.* Taylor's Weekend Gardening Guides. Boston: Houghton Mifflin, 1997.

**Westcott, Cynthia, and R. Kenneth Horst, eds.** *Westcott's Plant Disease Handbook.* New York: Springer Netherlands, 2008.

# USEFUL WEBSITES

## GENERAL INFORMATION

### NYBG LuEsther T. Mertz Library

*The New York Botanical Garden's Mertz Library is the most comprehensive botanical and horticultural library in the Americas. In addition to its extensive collections, the Mertz Library maintains a Plant Information Office, where the staff draws on the library's collections as well as their own professional experience to answer a variety of questions from the public related to plants. Popular topics include indoor and outdoor horticulture, with staff providing expertise in a variety of areas, from plant identification and integrated pest management to landscape and floral design. The service provides valuable information on cultural requirements, such as planting, fertilizing, pruning, and propagation, as well as assistance with landscape design inquiries. Home gardeners can reach the New York Botanical Garden Plant Information Service via phone or email, or through the website: "Ask an Expert," search "Gardening FAQs," and read numerous plant information and gardening guides.*

libguides.nybg.org/portalpage

### U.S. State Cooperative Extension System

*A wealth of reliable, research-based information can be found through the websites and county extension offices of the Cooperative Extension System, a part of the U.S. Department of Agriculture.*

*The Cooperative Extension System is a nationwide, noncredit educational network. Each U.S. state and territory has a state office at its land-grant university and a network of local or regional offices. These offices are staffed by one or more experts who provide useful, practical, and research-based information to agricultural producers, small business owners, youth, consumers, and others in rural areas and communities of all sizes. You can find the phone number for your Cooperative Extension Service office in the local government section of your telephone directory or through these websites:*

nifa.usda.gov/extension
extension.org/

## GARDEN CALENDARS

**Gardening Calendars for Indiana, Purdue University, Consumer Horticulture**

purdue.edu/hla/sites/yardandgarden/publication/gardening
-calendars/

**Seasonal Gardening Chores (New York Area)**

libguides.nybg.org/faqsspring
libguides.nybg.org/faqssummer
libguides.nybg.org/faqsfall
libguides.nybg.org/faqswinter

## GARDEN DESIGN AND LANDSCAPING

### COLOR IN THE GARDEN

**Landscape Basics: Color Theory, University of Georgia Cooperative Extension**

extension.uga.edu/publications/detail.cfm?number=B1396

### COMBINING PLANTS

**Plants in Combination, Missouri Botanical Garden**

www.missouribotanicalgarden.org/gardens-gardening/your
-garden/help-for-the-home-gardener/advice-tips-resources/
visual-guides/plants-in-combination.aspx

### GARDENING IN SMALL SPACES

**Grid Gardening, University of California, Davis**
ucanr.edu/sites/MarinMG/files/146810.pdf

## HOUSEPLANTS

Houseplants, University of Illinois Extension
extension.illinois.edu/houseplants/

## LANDSCAPING

Landscaping, University of Minnesota Extension
www.extension.umn.edu/garden/yard-garden/landscaping/

## HOW-TO TOPICS

### BIODYNAMIC FARMING AND GARDENING

Biodynamic Association
biodynamics.com

### HOUSEPLANT PROBLEMS

Preventing, Diagnosing, and Correcting Common Houseplant
Problems, Penn State Extension
extension.psu.edu/plants/gardening/fact-sheets/houseplants/
houseplant-problems

### LAWN CARE

The UC Guide to Healthy Lawns, University of California, Integrated
Pest Management Program
ipm.ucanr.edu/TOOLS/TURF/index.html

## ORGANIC GARDENING

**Organic Perennial Gardening and Pest Control, New York Botanical Garden**
libguides.nybg.org/aecontent.php?pid=622442&sid=5146918

**Organic Gardening, Cornell University**
gardening.cals.cornell.edu/files/2015/12/09organic-spag6n.pdf

**Using Organic Fungicides, Purdue University Extension**
extension.purdue.edu/extmedia/bp/bp-69-w.pdf

## PLANT DISEASE IN VEGETABLES

**Vegetable MD Online, Cornell University**
vegetablemdonline.ppath.cornell.edu

## SEED COLLECTING AND STORING

**An Introduction to Seed Saving for the Home Gardener, University of Maine Cooperative Extension**
extension.umaine.edu/publications/2750e/

## SEED SAVING

**Saving Seeds, Chicago Botanic Garden**
chicagobotanic.org/conservation/saving_seeds

## SOIL

**Soils and Composting: Soil Improvement, eXtension**
articles.extension.org/pages/13048/soils-and-composting:-soil
-improvement#.VE-vBfnrzA8

## SOIL MANAGEMENT

**Soil Health Management, U.S. Department of Agriculture, Natural Resources Conservation Service**

nrcs.usda.gov/wps/portal/nrcs/main/soils/health/mgnt/

## SOIL MAPS AND SOIL TAXONOMY DATABASE

**The Twelve Soil Orders: Soil Taxonomy, University of Idaho, College of Agricultural and Life Sciences**

cals.uidaho.edu/soilorders/

## PLANT INFORMATION

## ANNUALS AND PERENNIALS

**Beyond Impatiens and Petunias: Plant Directory, University of Illinois Extension**

extension.illinois.edu/beyond/directory.cfm

## FERNS

**American Fern Society**

amerfernsoc.org

## HERBS

**Herb Society of America**

herbsociety.org

## IRISES

**American Iris Society**

irises.org

## NATIVE PLANTS

Lady Bird Johnson Wildflower Center, University of Texas at Austin
Information about native plants and conservation
wildflower.org

## ORCHIDS

American Orchid Society
aos.org

## PLANT AND NURSERY FINDER

Plant Information Online, University of Minnesota
plantinfo.umn.edu

## PLANT DATABASE

Plants Database, U.S. Department of Agriculture
*Standardized information about the flowering and nonflowering plants of America*

plants.usda.gov/java/

## PLANT FACTS

Plant Facts, Ohio State University, Department of Horticulture and Crop Science
*Multimedia horticulture center with glossary, plant list, images, and videos*

plantfacts.osu.edu

## PLANT HARDINESS

Plant Hardiness Zone Map, USDA Agricultural Research Service
planthardiness.ars.usda.gov/PHZMWeb/

## PLANT IMAGES

**Image Gallery, U.S. Department of Agriculture, Natural Resources Conservation Service**

plants.usda.gov/gallery.html

## PLANT LIST

**List of all known plant species: a collaboration of Royal Botanic Garden,** Edinburgh; Kew; and Missouri Botanical Garden, with other reputable institutions, including New York Botanical Garden

*A respected resource for establishing accepted botanical names*

theplantlist.org

**PlantFacts Plant List, Ohio State University, Department of Horticulture and Crop Science**

plantfacts.osu.edu/plantlist/

## ROSES

**HelpMe Find Roses, HelpMe Find.com**
*An online guide to over 44,000 rose cultivars and their growers*

helpmefind.com/rose/index.php

## TREES

**Tree Encyclopedia / North American Insects and Spiders**
*Over 450 species of North American trees described and photographed*

cirrusimage.com/wp/trees/

### GARDEN SUPPLIES

Gardener's Supply Company, based in Vermont, employee-owned company offering home gardeners information and garden supplies

gardeners.com

### HEIRLOOM SEEDS AND PLANTS

Seed Savers Exchange, whose mission is to collect, grow, and share heirloom seeds and plants

seedsavers.org

### NATIVE PLANTS

PlantNative website, with how-to information and a directory of suppliers and professionals

plantnative.org

### PLANT INFORMATION ONLINE

University of Minnesota website to locate plants from over 1,100 North American nurseries

plantinfo.umn.edu

*To inquire about suppliers of individual plants that you have not been able find through conventional sources, use the "Ask an Expert" feature on the New York Botanical Garden Plant Information Service website.*

libguides.nybg.org/portalpage

### VEGETABLE GARDENING

Illinois Vegetable Garden Guide, University of Illinois Extension

web.extension.illinois.edu/vegguide/

Seed for the Garden, Virginia Cooperative Extension

pubs.ext.vt.edu/426/426-316/426-316.html

## MY SUPPLIERS AND SOURCES